A BRIEF INTRODUCTION TO THE DEVELOPMENT OF DOCTRINE

According to the Mind of St. Thomas Aquinas

Fr. Thomas Gilby, O.P.

Scholastic Answers Press

CONTENTS

FOREWORD

In the period of Second Scholasticism (16th-17th century), there was a debate concerning the development of doctrine that many have never heard of. On the one side, there was Francisco Suárez, and on the other were the famed Discalced Carmelites of Salamanca (the *Salmanticenses*). The debate was over whether theological conclusions could be defined as dogmas.

Before this, theologians were (nearly) unanimous in affirming that theological conclusions could be defined as dogmas. The only debate was between the Scotists/Nominalists and the Thomists over *when* the transition from theological conclusion to dogma happened. Thomists held that a theological conclusion only became dogmatic *after* the definition of the Church. The Scotists/Nominalists held that the theological conclusion is dogmatic *before* the definition of the Church.

A quip from Domingo Báñez illustrates the traditional Thomistic position, "If anyone should confess that Christ is a perfect man, but deny that he is *risible* [i.e., have the ability to laugh] in the belief that risibility does not pertain to the perfection of man, **he would be a bad philosopher, but not yet a heretic**, since up to now the Church has not defined that Christ is risible. But if the Church were to define that risibility belongs to the perfection of human nature, as she has defined that Christ has two wills, divine and human, then anyone who denies that Christ is risible would be a heretic." (*In Partem Primam*, q.l, a.2, *ad tertium argumentum*)

Yet, due to innovations posited by Suarez, a third and fourth position are formed, causing many Thomists to depart from the teaching of the Angelic Doctor and his school.

In order to combat the dangerous theory of Suarez on this matter (the theory of continuing revelation), the *Salmanticenses* decided to do what only one theologian in the history of Catholic thought had done before (Luis de Molina) and denied that theological conclusions had *ever* been defined in the history of the Church or even could be done.

In the 20th century, this debate came to the forefront again. This time, within the Dominican Order. On the one hand, we have Fr. Francisco Marín-Sola, on the other, Fr. Réginald-Marie Schultes. The latter followed the "conservative" line of the *Salmanticenses,* the former went back to the teaching of St. Thomas Aquinas and the 16th century Thomists to resolve the issue.

It was in *this* debate that the heart of the issue was reached, i.e., what does it mean for a conclusion to be *virtually contained* in its premises. Fr. Marín-Sola rightly discerned that Suárez had "poisoned the well" on the issue by wrongly distinguishing between, what he called, *formal confused* (which he wrongly defined as that which is objectively identical) and *virtual* (which he wrongly defined as that which is objectively distinct).

Fr. Marín-Sola pointed out that for St. Thomas, St. Bonaventure, and the rest of the scholastic tradition (before Suarez), the distinction was **not** over objective identity, **but** over whether it is merely *notionally* distinct (as the difference between *man* and *rational animal,* which would be formal) and that which is objectively identical, yet, *conceptually* distinct WITH A FOUNDATION IN THE THING (as the difference between *rational animal* and *risible* which would be virtual).

Thus, when the *Salmanticenses* approached this issue on Suarez's terms, they clearly saw the danger in affirming a definition of a doctrine that is *objectively* distinct from that which is revealed and rightly condemned his position. Yet, they did not perceive where the problem truly lay. Rather than distinguishing between *notional* (formal) and *conceptual* (virtual) distinctions as their forebearers had done, they simply denied that theological conclusions could be defined.

Those in English speaking Catholicism are completely unaware of these debates streching back centuries (some even believe that St. John Henry Newman was the first to invent the development of doctrine). It was my joy to find, within an appendix of the *Gilby Summa,* what amounts to a compendium of Fr. Marín-Sola's teaching on this issue, with due recourse to the text of St. Thomas (as one can certainly gather from the endnotes).

Thus, this work becomes the perfect antidote to those English speaking Catholics who have only heard of the Development of Doctrine in terms of Newman, but never in terms of Aquinas.

-Christian B. Wagner

Feast of St. Thomas Aquinas, 2023

INTRODUCTION

Revelation is not oracular. It is the giving of God's Word in Christ to the body of Christ and there received in faith. [1] Propositions do not descend on us from heaven ready made, but are formed from the Church's thinking about this gift, and thinking aloud. This utterance or articulation is more a draft of work in progress than a final and completed document, for faith itself, though rooted in immutable truth, is not crowning knowledge, and its elaboration in teaching, namely theology, is still more bound up with discourses progressively manifesting fresh truths or fresh aspects of the truth to the mind. So the individual Christian and the Christian community grow in understanding; indeed they must if, like other living organisms, they are to survive by adaptation to a changing environment of history, ideas, and social pressures.

Nevertheless the governing rule, insisted on by Scripture and Tradition, is that the common revelation of what we should believe and do in order to be saved was completed by Christ, and suffers no addition until the glory to come that shall be revealed in us. [2] Hold this firm, says St Thomas when commenting on the text, one Lord, one faith, one baptism, [3] that the faith of the ancients and the modems is identical, otherwise the Church would not be one. [4]

THE GENERAL
PROBLEM

Little effort of historical imagination is required to admit how puzzled an early Christian would have been had he been presented with a preview of the Council of Nicea, and how St Peter himself might have suspended belief had the infallibility formula of the first Vatican Council been put to him abstractly; St Thomas [a] observed no [explicit] mention of a defined Trinitarian doctrine [i.e., the notions] in Holy Scripture. [5] Nevertheless assent to dogmas previously not binding has been made a condition of remaining in the visible unity of the Church-how then do we escape the curse on those who preach what is besides the gospel we have received and additional to the words of prophecy? [6]

The difficulty, which differs in degree but not in kind for Christians who inherit nineteen centuries of doctrinal development and those who stop with the first four General Councils or even earlier, is perhaps only to be avoided by a group that performed the impossible anachronism of reproducing the exact color and tone of the convictions, hopes, fears, sentiments, and devotions of the Apostolic Age and of insulating itself against the influences of any other culture. The Gospel is for all time and works like a ferment in the mass, and the difficulty has to be faced, particularly by those who would think of the Church, not as the enzyme, but as the end product. Somehow the canon of St. Vincent of Lerins, *we hold what has been believed everywhere, always, and by everybody*, has to be combined with [his statement that is included in the first Vatican Council], that *there is an increase, though always in the same meaning and the same judgment.* [7]

The purpose of this [work] is to consider the terms in which scholastic theology couches this development. We shall, therefore, keep to the metier of treating the process as a progression of propositions. In revelation we encounter the presence of God in a mystery deeper than the statements about him which also confront us, and which involve words. [8] Similarly, the Church's life grows by ever-renewed contact with the living Christ, not directly by increasingly detailed and systematic thinking about him. All the same, thinking is involved together with its verbal expression in teaching, and this is properly subject to logic.

Clearly there are accretions in what may be called the cultural surround to revelation in the Church;

these, which are matters of more immediate interest to the social psychologist and historian of religion than to the theologian, vary with periods and regions; the preoccupations they give rise to are reflected in different mental tempers, styles of worship, literatures of devotion, and modes of administration. Some of them can loom very large, and periodically the Church has to reduce them to their proper proportions; the theologian can view them with respect mingled with a certain detachment since, unlike the historical moralist, he has no preference for one period over another. He looks for the living Gospel as confidently in Trent as in the Didache, and most contemporaneously in the current teaching of the Church.

The plain facts of history show that Christian doctrine has developed under the influences of philosophies, cultures, and civilizations. For the explanation much will depend on how far these are regarded as strange to living with God and consequently lying outside God's plan for our salvation. Obviously a theology, such as St Thomas's, which literally would restore all things in Christ will approach the problem differently from a theology less genial about the presence of nature in the kingdom of grace.

IMPLICIT AND VIRTUAL

Despite their general agreement, a difference of emphasis can be discerned when the scholastic theologians come to describe the development. To some it is a passage which renders *explicit* what previously was only *implicitly* stated; to others it is a passage which renders *actual* what previously was only *virtually* present. The terms need not be pressed too exclusively, for on occasion St Thomas treats *implicit* and *virtual* content as equivalent. [9] All the same an effect which is implied is not quite the same as an effect which a cause is capable of producing; so that *virtual,* when applied to inference, suggests that a stronger effort of reasoning is required to bring it out; this may go to account for the preference of the hardier logicians among the theologians, who choose to speak of a developed religious truth being *virtually,* not merely *implicitly,* contained in the principles of faith. The two terms, however, stand for shades of difference in a single process, for if implicit presence be taken to signify what is involved though not necessarily stated, then it is well shown that Christian truth keeps its identity throughout its progressive manifestations, and if virtual presence be taken to signify what is really in the principle though not yet elicited, then it is well shown that fresh conclusions can be produced in our minds.

For that is where the development takes place; it is a growth of manifestation and of explanation, *explicatio*, **not** of the substance of revelation or of the deposit of faith. To theologians who are content to describe the growth as an unfolding of what has been accepted, and who look to the content rather than to the articulation of faith, the reply to the question, "Would St Peter himself have believed in the infallibility of pronouncements *ex cathedra*?" would be, yes. To others, more preoccupied with the logic, and therefore the propositional forms, of development, the question, whether he would have subscribed to the terms of the Vatican decree, becomes rather unreal. This is a case of the *a priori* happily helping the empirical spirit; not that the great scholastics, who cast the problem in this second mode, are conspicuous for their sense of history, but that they are saved from anachronism by their sense of proportion about how the human mind works and their exact appreciation of what logical advance entails. An account of their teaching provides a useful chart for reference, besides extending St Thomas's conception of theology as science.

EVOLUTION
OF DOGMAS

Theories of evolution were less engrossing in the Middle Ages than they are now; despite the increase of doctrine and law, the Church of the time was most set on maintaining its apostolic foundations against enthusiasts who preached the coming of the Kingdom of the Spirit. St Thomas does little more than lay down the main principles of doctrinal evolution. Like other scholastic masters he treated the *explicatio fidei* or *explicatio articulorum fidei* at two places, namely when considering first, the identity of faith under the Old and New Testaments, and second, the Church's power to determine the rule of faith binding under pain of heresy and separation from its body.

The initial inquiry is directed to the continuity of faith between Israel and the Christian Church, but the answers take account of the development of dogma since the time of our Lord: St Thomas seems to have had no great sense of distance in time, but speaks familiarly of Aristotle and St Augustine as though they were contemporaries, and refers to William of Auxerre and Philip the Chancellor, both of whom died when he was a boy, as *antiqui*. The longest treatment is found in his Commentary on the Sentences, the most compressed in the Disputations, and the most careful in the *Summa*. [13]

Behind his treatment lies the distinction between the substance and the statement of faith. The first lies in the object itself outside us, *extra animam*, and this is the incomplex and unchanging reality of God; so faith is one, as is any power, habit, or activity bent on one object. [15] The second is the object as accepted and shared by the human subject, *in acceptatione nostra, participatum in cognoscente*, and in this partaking faith is multiplied, *plurificatur*, in diverse pronouncements or propositions, *enuntiabilia*.

The basic truth of faith is God's being and providence for human salvation he that cometh to God must believe that he is, and that he is a rewarder of them that diligently seek him. [16] The divine being, *divinum esse*, includes all that is believed to exist eternally in God, and divine providence includes all temporal affairs he arranges for his glory in our happiness. These two cover all the subsequent articles of faith, "in the same way that faith in our Redeemer implicitly holds faith in the Incarnation and the passion and other mysteries of Christ." [17] He goes on, "here there is no enlargement during the course of centuries, but whatever those coming after have believed was contained, though implicitly, in the faith of the Patriarchs who came before them. Yet as regards its explication, the number of articles has grown, for some things are explicitly known now which were not so known by earlier generations. So the Lord spoke to Moses, *I am the God of Abraham, the God of Isaac, the God of Jacob, but by my name Adonai was I not known to them.* And St Paul speaks of the mystery of Christ, *which in other ages was not made known unto the sons of men, as it is now revealed unto his holy apostles and prophets by the Spirit.*"

It will be noticed that St Thomas has almost imperceptibly brought forward the enduring unity of faith from the underlying object to the first affirmation of the believer; the substance of faith has become the substance of the articles of faith. The fundamental affirmation of faith stands to later affirmations as the first principle of thought, namely the principle of contradiction, stands to later philosophical statements. [20] The comparison may be extended, for as the sole inspection of the principle of contradiction provides no conclusion for metaphysics, still less for the other sciences, so assent to the basic truth of faith needs to be joined to another assent, whether to an acknowledged deed of God or a solemn decision of Christ's Church or (as we shall see presently) a minor premise of indubitable reason, if it is to issue into assent to more determinately Christian truths. So that when the term "implicit" is used in the formula to explain the identity between primitive faith and its subsequent developments it offers little heuristic help to show how the first grows into the second.

Indeed the term is applied of the New Testament in relation to the Old Testament. The Father is Yahweh, and the divine mysteries revealed in Christ in themselves were implicit in God's dealings with man from the beginning. Yet to the human mind they were only adumbrated, and scarcely implicit. [21] Revelation itself grew with new truths until in the fullness of time it was completed, so far as was needed for God's economy of man's salvation, in Christ. So that now all the truths of faith are implicitly present for us in the Apostolic teaching, from which it is not lawful to subtract and to which it is not lawful to add. [22]

All the same advance is still possible, and St Thomas then points to the two ways that lie open, corresponding to the two passages already noted, the first from *implicit* to *explicit,* the second from *virtual* to *actual.* The first is present when an article of faith is included in another, *in alio*, or is an integral part of the common ground of faith and so is included *in uno communi*; thus the resurrection of the dead is held in the resurrection of Christ, and the mysteries of Christ's life, death, and resurrection are held in the whole mystery of the Atonement. This way of proceeding offers less theoretic difficulty than the second way, since the process looks like **immediate inference** and remains within the complex of the truths of faith.

In the second way, however, the start is from an article or articles of faith, not taken narrowly and precisely in themselves (if that be possible), but as invested or associated with a truth that goes with them, *concomitans articulum*, namely a truth that also has meaning outside the Christian context. Thus the essential attributes of human nature are discussed by philosophical psychology, apart from their being taken into the theological discourse which, starting from the principle of faith that God became man, proceeds to conclusions about Christ, for instance that he enjoyed human freewill. Along this way faith can be extended continuously, *quotidie*, and has been by the learned studies of Doctors of the Church, *per studium sanctorum magis et magis explicata*. [24]

This process of exposition leads to theological conclusions by **mediate inference** in which a term can be made to look as though it were derived from profane, not sacred, sources; for instance, an essential attribute of human nature according to philosophical psychology. This, however, is to make an abstraction that is not to the point, for the meaning of the term is not added to the truth revealed from outside, but goes with it, *concomitans*. For revelation does not give us a separated form divested of all save a purely supernatural meaning;

if such a naked supernatural concept could exist it would still have to include a reference to its matter, [27] in this case its rational meaning to the receiving subject, which is the natural mind and not some newly created and specially supernatural faculty. Let us not pursue these unreal speculations about a supernatural quality without a natural substance, or an assent without a thought or a thought without an image and a word, but repeat instead, that by revelation the Word of God is embodied in us. A supernatural meaning is not like a core, round which natural meanings and images can cluster, but like the soul, whole and entire in every part of the body it animates. [29] Indeed it is gracious, and therefore also natural. A philosophical term loses nothing, but admits a fresh meaning in the light of revelation when taken into the discourse of theology; and, as we shall see, such notions as "essential property" and "cause" become richer mines of thought.

Note further that articles of faith can be assertions of historical fact, and that accordingly they are developed not merely by a logic based on the inspection of meanings but also by the continued showing of God's might and mercy in Christ through his Church. They are not just truths, but saving truths; they are not evident in the light of reason, but accepted in the darkness of faith; assent to them is a binding condition, not for intellectual consistency, but for our living in the unity of

Christ's body. The articulations of thinking faith in the individual are true less because he can trace all their logical connections than because they are resonant of the thoughts ever growing in the mind of the Church.

St Thomas refers to an opinion ventilated in the schools which, attempting to show the identity of faith between Israel and the Church, held that a truth could be lifted out of the time-series, since it is, as it were, accidental to faith in the Messiah whether he is still to come or has come. [32] On the contrary, faith is an assent that may have to pin itself to an historical event; "suffered under Pontius Pilate, the third day rose again from the dead." The historic Christ is a fixed point for faith in the Incarnation, and this is future to those who came before him, past to those who come after. [33]

For divine revelation is not received as a pure form without matter or genealogy, as if men were spirits out of place and time or spirits imprisoned in bodies and now given a message of escape. As for their essential wholeness they require matter, and for their integrity members, and for their personality individual accidents, so revelation comes to them compact of fact and human experience. "Hence it should be declared that in an article of faith which is the object of faith as judged, *objectum fidei complexum*, there is something material, for instance Christ's passion, something formal, namely God's reality, and something accidental,

15

namely that it took place at a certain time." [34]

Consequently, whatever the nature of doctrinal development the process, unlike that of idealist metaphysics or pure mathematics, will not be confined to working from abstract essences to their necessary implications. When "perfect man" is taken as a starting point in Christological argument this is not the ideal man of moral philosophy, but a historic man full of grace and truth, of whose fullness we have all received, [35] who came to us from no inner necessity of things, but to redeem us, the propitiation for the sins of the whole world, [36] by the will of God whose free acts cannot be deduced from any principle, whose mighty power raised him from the dead and hath put all things under his feet and gave him to be the head over all things. [37] None of these things are evident in themselves, nor can they be taken back to anything we see; they are accepted by faith because of God's word declared to us and not because they are recommended by our sense of the reasonable.

On two counts, then, Christian theology breaks out of the limits imposed on an abstract science: first, because its data are what divine omnipotence and mercy have done beyond the ordinary course of justice and benevolence, and second, because they have been done in historic time. [38] Neither acts of generosity nor historic events can be resolved by the human mind into a binding principle; neither, therefore, can be demonstrated. So faith comes from listening, not from seeing, from taking what is offered, not from proving it. [39] If the theology which develops from this assent be called an imperfect kind of science then let it pass, with the reflection that the same may be said of literature and the deepest kinds of knowledge.

HERESY

This quality of assent to a truth because it is declared to us, not because we discover it, descends into our attitude towards the authoritative witness of the Church, which has the office, not only of conserving what is given in revelation, but also of explaining it, so far as is possible and fitting, in terms of the current ideas and sympathies of the faithful, by determining what statements are authentically in the tradition and what devotions are salutary, in other words, by regulating the rule of faith and worship.

Before considering the scope of this office it should be noted that we believe God because of God and nothing less, that the inner cause, or formal motive as it is called, of faith is his Word and his revelation, and that the testimony of the Church is not the reason why we believe but the ordinary medium in which we discover what determinate truths have been revealed. For faith *stands on the power of God*, [40] and is in *the gospel which is the power of God unto salvation unto everybody who believes*; [41]

it is *Jesus who is the author and finisher of faith*, [42] and the influence of the Church here is that of bringing our minds to bear, *causa applicans*, on the riches of revelation. Hence there is no vicious circle of believing the Church because of Revelation and believing Revelation because of the Church. Nevertheless the role of the Church is decisive in shaping the course of theological discourse and determining what propositions are to be held or rejected.

This guardianship attends the growing articulation of the principal truths of faith, and is given such power that, as St Thomas notes, many things are now judged to be heretical which previously were not. [43] Heresy is that species of infidelity which would lop off branches rather than strike at the root of Christian faith. It assents to Christ as an end, but fails with the means he has instituted, for its choices are erected by private judgment against the living tradition: heretics are those who profess faith in Christ but would destroy the dogmas, or some of them. [44] Heresy consists in opposing in the name of Christianity the rule of faith authoritatively proposed by the contemporary Church. It is a nonconformity to the doctrinal order, an irregularity within the Christian scene, an ambivalence with respect to the total integrity of faith, accepting one part but disbelieving another. For truths belong to faith in two ways, says St Thomas, directly and principally, for instance the Trinity and the Incarnation, or indirectly and secondarily, for instance the reliability of Holy Scripture, in which the articles of faith are involved. Both classes of truth are covered by the virtue of faith, and both can be attacked by a contrary vice. [45]

Nevertheless only under special conditions does the denial of a secondary truth amount to heresy, and St Thomas proceeds very cautiously when deciding what these circumstances are. Formal heresy, after all, is a gravely culpable disbelief, more than doubt or wavering or unbelief or a modestly expressed misjudgment; a person may be tottering into heresy and not be there. It is an opinion maintained fanatically and stubbornly, *vehementer et pertinaciter*, above all it is a social act, a separation from communion in the Church's teaching. [46] No authority in the world apart from the Church can decide what secondary propositions are so bound up with the central truths of revelation that their denial would be against the due profession of the Christian faith. Respect will be expected and obedience may be enjoined with regard to other propositions that are put forward in the exercise of the Church's office to safeguard Christian faith and morals, but only when it is so stated are they binding *de fide*.

Propositions against the articles of faith are censured as heretical, propositions against the theological conclusions which can be drawn from them, but which are not solemnly defined, may be condemned as erroneous. The descending gamut of censures is: openly (*notorie*) heretical, proximate to heresy (*hæresi proxima*), smacking of heresy (*hæresim sapiens*), suspiciously like heresy (*suspecta de hæresi*); plainly erroneous, close to error, smacking of error, suspiciously like error. (Being close to heresy or error is deviating from the common teaching, *communis sententia*; smacking of heresy or error is providing a handle, *ansa*, for fears on that score; suspicion marks a tendency without proceeding to the unfair judgment condemned in ST.II-II.Q60.A3) Then propositions may be censured as rash (*temeraria*) when doctrinal statements are made without solid support, badly put (*male sonans*) when the sense but not the words are acceptable, sophistical (*captiosa*) when exception cannot be taken to the words but the sense is deceiving. Propositions may also be condemned as blasphemous, schismatic, scandalous, or offensive. Blasphemy is against the profession of faith, but as derogating from God's goodness and some times as a detesting of what is believed offends more against the lovingness than the formal teaching of faith (cf. ST.II-II.Q13.A3). Schism, which is numbered among the vices directly opposed to charity, attacks the unity of the Church (cf. ST.II-II.Q39.A2-3). To give scandal is not to shock but to be a stumbling block to others to give occasion for their spiritual harm (ST.II-II.Q43.A3). Offensiveness may range from sacrilege (ST.II-II.Q99) to bickering (ST.II-II.Q116).

Private sins against faith are a more flexible matter. There is always the duty of being in sympathy with the whole body, though *sentire cum Ecclesia* is not the same as following the dominant party-line. Moreover, what may be called the detailed coverage of faith will vary from person to person according to differences of intelligence, learning, and professional office. Some will perceive more implications and greater subtleties in the gospel which is preached to all; they must follow the light of the Spirit along lonelier tracks and perhaps suffer special occupational temptations; if they are teachers a greater elaboration of faith may be required of them. [48]

LOGIC OF DEVELOPMENT

To turn now to the logic of the development of doctrine. Observe as a preliminary, first, that this section touches only the framework of the subject, and second, that the framework is that of the Aristotelian syllogism.

First, logic is a thinking about thoughts, and not for their real significance but for their coherence together. It is concerned with the correct use of terms, propositions, and arguments among themselves, not with their relevance to real life which is the concern of other disciplines. Consequently when scholastic theologians seem preoccupied merely with the formal pattern of doctrinal development it should not be thought that they are substituting it for the living growth observed by biblical and historical studies, though some of them, like many specialists, may give the impression of being addicted to the apparatus.

Secondly, the logic adopted as convenient for their

purpose is the Aristotelian logic which works with the identities or non-identities predicated between terms, for they are engaged in showing that theological conclusions, notably those that become articles of faith, are somehow contained in the premises of revelation. The medievals constructed another logic beyond Aristotle's as in the last hundred years men have constructed another logic beyond theirs; yet the scholastics found the old classical logic sufficient for their purpose. It is not obsolete, and offers a useful plan when the development of doctrine is treated as a series of inferences from a group of propositions held by faith.

The logical structure of the body of truths proposed for our salvation is a matter not only of interest but also of devotion, as appears from the writings of the classical scholastics, and not least those who might be termed high and dry. Cajetan is an eminent example; the virtuosity of his logic expresses the confidence that faith can enter the whole life of reasoning as charity can enter the whole life of loving. We have already remarked the same quality in St Thomas who does not, as it were, put on a church face when he turns from profane to sacred topics. It was the same confidence; *all things are yours, and you are Christ's, and Christ is God's.* [49]

So the holy teaching, as we have seen, is composed of human elements. The question is, are they alien elements to divine revelation, additions to what has been given us, so that the product, the theological conclusion, is a hybrid of grace and nature, and the evolution of doctrine is transformist and heterogeneous? Or are these elements essentially contained in a single subject and a single situation, namely men together in the plan of God's saving mercy, so that the product runs true to type, namely nature uplifted by grace, and the evolution is homogeneous? The school of St Thomas adopts the second of these alternatives; in agreement grace and nature, like spirit and body, can combine in one. Neither at best represent pre-established harmonies that never really meet nor at worst antagonistic forces that fight it out on the battlefield of man.

Four parts may be distinguished in the complex body of truths proposed to us by the Church, namely a. the gift revealed in Scripture, to reject which is infidelity; b. the dogmas or articles of faith defined by the Church, to reject which is heresy; c. theological conclusions or necessary inferences from the truths of faith, the denial of which may be censured as erroneous; d. dogmatic facts, or that historical setting to theological statements which has to be accepted if these are to have any force, for instance that Jansenism really was found in the Augustinus, that Pius IX was a lawful pope, and that the First Vatican Council was ecumenical.

A fifth class, sometimes added, is here neglected since as regards the development of dogma its condition resembles that of (c); it includes truths, especially moral truths, accepted by the Church but not defined as parts of revelation. [b]

Now this is not a classification of separate elements each in its own compartment, but of different phases in or abstracts from the single process of growing in the knowledge and love of God. The truths are not so fixed in their categories that they cannot communicate and transfer; there is no restriction of divine faith to *a* and *b*, leaving *c* and *d* to be covered by what is called ecclesiastical faith. The situation is more open, for divine faith in *a* takes the others in its stride. Indeed, as we have seen, divine revelation is not to be isolated in some mysterious and spiritual communication but to be extended into the physical and social life of God's people. From the Word (a) made flesh (b) flow meanings (c) in time (d), and the progression from *a* to *d* is continuous.

So St Thomas speaks of a thing open to *sacra doctrina* because it is *revelabile*, that is because it can enter the field of revelation; he does not apply the narrower test of its being expressly revealed, *revelatum*. [53] Reference to every article of the first question of the Summa on *sacra doctrina* shows how wide is this field, for the supernatural mystery of God covers also the natural truths of religion, [54] historical facts accessory to revelation, [55] human acts, [56] philosophical truths, [57] the critique of them, [58] the historic Christ, [59] the rules of logic, [60] the proper use of metaphor, [61] and the principles of literary interpretation. [62]

Our present inquiry is directed on the logic of development from *b* to *c*, that is from an article of faith to a theological conclusion, in order that light may be thrown on the historical development whereby *c* becomes *b* by the defining power of the Church. This sharpening of a truth of faith by philosophy appears in the General Councils, beginning with Nicea which declared that the Son was one substance, not like substance, with the Father, going on to Ephesus, which declared that Mary was God-bearer, not merely Christ-bearer, and the third Council of Constantinople, which declared that there are two wills in Christ, and so continuing until our time. The Church has always thought what St. Athanasius said about Nicea, that the word of the Lord set forth by the Council is an eternal word enduring forever, although as in the examples given, of the first, third, and sixth ecumenical councils, the definitions against Arianism, Nestorianism, and Monothelitism involved philosophical concepts. [63] It is clear that a conclusion arrived at by thinking about the faith must be very close to the faith itself if it can be made a condition of communion with the Church. How close will appear when the development is read according to the categories of scholastic logic. [64]

Let two statements be taken to represent the contrast between a primitive confession of faith and a reflection on it in technical terms; first the words of St Thomas Didymus, *My Lord and my God*, [66] and next the words of St Thomas Aquinas, *the honor of worship is properly due to a subsistent hypostasis, and on this account our worship of Christ's humanity and flesh because of the thing there is the worship due to the Incarnate Word and therefore is latria.* [66] How different the ring and simplicity of the one from the scholasticism of the other, how different the concepts and terms, how different the temper, yet both convey the same underlying truth of judgment. Recall that truth in the human mind is not constituted by the apprehension of an impression or a likeness or species, but by an act of judgment bearing on the existing world, that this is that or this is not that. [67] That being the case, we have to listen less to the ring of the words than to the real meanings they make together, and look less to the literary figure than to the deeper theological form: otherwise we may discern little continuity between Sinai and Galilee, the Jerusalem of Solomon and of the apostles meeting together, the Ephesus of St. Paul and of the Council, between Chalcedon and Vienne, Florence and Trent. The better to understand the simultaneous sameness and difference in the elaboration of revelation through the development of dogma let us turn to the scholastic treatment of *distinction* before applying it to the concepts, judgments, and reasonings of a living and growing *sacra doctrina.* [68]

PROGRESS FROM ONE TO ANOTHER

In the intricacies of the logic there is no general agreement, yet the following outline will not be disputed in the main. Distinction, the opposite of identity, signifies a plurality of terms; one is not another. It may be objective or subjective. Objective or real distinction, *distinctio realis*, expresses a non-identity the mind discovers in things, either between distinct things or complete substances, e.g. Peter and Paul, or between distinct principles in one thing, e.g. Peter's body and soul. Subjective or mental distinction, *distinctio rationis*, expresses a non-identity the mind reads into things. It is of two kinds, conceptual or virtual distinction, *distinctio rationis ratiocinatae*, when the concepts are not identical, e.g. spiritual being and immortal being, and purely nominal or logical distinction, *distinctio rationis ratiocinantis*, when at a further remove from reality only the words used are not identical, e.g.

equilateral and equiangular triangle.

For brevity and with some warrant in scholastic usage let us take these four types of distinction as referring to objects that are respectively diverse, different, distinctive, and merely nominally distinct. Terms and propositions are diverse when they signify distinct individual things, [69] different when they signify distinct realities which however do not exist in themselves but only together, [70] distinctive when they signify distinct meanings which however are later admitted to come to the same thing, [71] and merely nominally distinct when they signify an identical meaning modified only by a circumstance of grammar or language. [72]

Next let us apply these four types of distinction first to the discourse of reasoning using a process of elimination, and next to the development of doctrine. A conclusion arrived at may be diverse from its principle, or add a real difference to it, or introduce a distinctive note, or find a new formula but not a new idea.

This last we can eliminate at once, since reasoning properly so-called is a movement of ideas, not merely of words, leading to a conclusion that is new knowledge not merely a restatement of old knowledge. Theological development marks more than an advance in terminology behind which the concepts remain fixed. Furthermore, the process does more than elucidate concepts, such as happens when the seeming conclusion is presupposed in the premises as an essential part in the whole or a particular in an unconditional universal or a correlative in its opposite number. In the syllogism of science, including the science of theology, the passage through the middle term is one of thought, not merely of language [c].

Yet at the other extreme we must also eliminate the first type of progression [d], namely when the truth of the conclusion adds a diverse element to the premise. And for two reasons, firstly because such progression is proper to the natural and practical sciences, not to the properly philosophical and theological sciences. The argument ranges outside the meaning of the principle of meaning and associates it with a judgment of fact verified by observation or experiment; consequently the conclusion, though connected with the principle, is not implicitly or virtually contained there; its certainty is conditional on the truth of the second judgment of fact. [73] Secondly, because the development of Christian doctrine requires no outside element to be introduced, and indeed permits no addition to be made to what is contained in revelation. To add, remarks St Thomas, may be either adding something contrary or diverse-and this is erroneous or presumptuous-explaining what is implicitly contained-and this is praiseworthy. [74]

Next, the second type of progression can also be eliminated, and for much the same reason. For here the principle is like a genus which by the addition of a specific diference forms a species, and though the species "human being" is in a sense contained in the genus "animal being," it is only by transformist or heterogeneous evolution (whatever the proximate causes) that animal becomes human. Similarly in other cases as well where the resultant or consequent is really different from its principle. [75] Revelation and the first principles of faith, however, produce conclusions from within themselves; all that is developed is included from the beginning in the *revelabile*, [76] and there is no accretion.

We are left therefore with the third type of progression, namely when principle and term are virtually distinct, or what we have called distinctive. The conclusion is implicitly or virtually contained in the principle yet requires to be elicited by a conceptual advance. This is the process of *scientia* in its strictest Aristotelian science; it is not performed by the mere inspection of concepts in the major premise, but requires the further judgment that one of the concepts there expressed (the middle term) is to be identified or not with a third concept, and this because of their very meaning and not because they are observed to be always or nearly always associated in fact. From these two judgments a third follows, namely the conclusion.

Appreciate that the conclusion is at once implicit in the premises and distinctive in itself, and then the appropriateness of this style of reasoning to

Christian doctrine will be recognized. For theology promises no discovery of fresh territory on this side of the grave, but rather the consolidation and exploitation of what is already accepted from revelation. The reasoning, unlike that of the natural sciences, does not really advance beyond its first understanding, but seeks to enlarge that understanding; the closeness of the two functions of understanding and reasoning should be particularly evident in theology.

The discourse of reason always begins from an understanding and ends at an understanding; because we reason by proceeding from certain understood principles, and the discourse of reason is perfected when we come to understand what hitherto we ignored. Hence the act of reasoning proceeds from something previously understood. Now a gift of grace does not proceed from the light of nature, but is added thereto as perfecting it. Wherefore this addition is not called reason but understanding, since the additional light is in comparison with what we know supernaturally, what the natural light is in regard to those things which we know from the first. [78]

Recall also that while the articles of faith serve as the first principles of theological science, [79] they are in themselves as propositions no more ultimate than are the first principles of reason; both are responses of the human mind to the reality it conceives and bears, the former to the truth of God himself, *veritas prima*, the latter to the truth of being, *ens ut verum*.

What is revealed is God, not a set of propositions. Systematic theology makes even less claim to cage divine truth than systematic philosophy to capture the essences of material things. Nevertheless we have to speak the truth in our manner, and as faith is articulated in articles which are like principles so these principles in their turn are developed into conclusions.

As God, since he knows himself, knows in a way that is his own, that is, by simple intuition, not by discursive thought, so we, from those truths that we possess in adhering to First Truth, come to a knowledge of other truths, according to our own mode of cognition, namely, by proceeding from principles to conclusions. Wherefore, those truths that we hold in the first place by faith are for us, as it were, first principles in this science, and the other truths to which we attain are quasi-conclusions. [80]

So much for the closeness of conclusions to principles; now for their distinctness. It will be well to notice how the third type of argumentative progression works under different conditions when Christian dogma is developed and when the mathematical and metaphysical sciences infer conclusions from their premises. What is common is that a deduction of property from essence or of effect from cause may be represented; what is different is that *essence* and *cause* or their equivalents are not the same for philosophy and for theology.

"ESSENTIAL PROPERTY" IN THEOLOGICAL DISCOURSE

Essence here means no more than what the subject is defined to be. [81] That subject is the whole matter of the inquiry. [82] A whole, *totum*, implies parts at least conceptually distinct, [83] and for our present purposes may be divided into an essential whole, *totum essentiale*, an integral whole, *totum integrale*, and a whole combination of powers, *totum potestativum*. [84] An essential whole contains the specific attributes or essential properties of a thing, thus from "rational animal" as an essential whole may be inferred freewill, imagination, and a sense of humor-all at least as aptitudes. An integral whole contains also the normal requirements for the essential whole to be realized, thus "rational animal" will require a pair of hands and two feet. A whole as a combination of powers can be pushed to the fullest expansion of which it is capable, and a whole at full power in the case of man will include every perfection to which human nature can be taken by grace, thus thus to be sinless and beyond suffering and death. Accordingly we can draw a distinction between pure essence, or the universal nature of a thing, integral essence, or the thing in its connatural condition, and perfect essence, or the thing with every power realized. The first is implicit in the second and can be inferred from it; the second is implicit in the third, and can be inferred from it.

Let us continue with the example we have chosen of the essence 'man'. Philosophical theory can infer with certainty some conclusions from human nature as such, that is from the pure essence, but its touch is much less certain when dealing with the integral essence or human nature as adapted to environment, for then it has to move from its own realm of necessary reasons and can cut an absurd figure if it dogmatizes about facts and fails to consult the whole range of historical and anthropological sciences. But neither philosophical theory nor these other sciences can reach to the perfect essence of man, as revealed in Jesus Christ, *full of grace and truth, of whose fullness we have all received,* [85] *the head of all principality and power,* [86] *and to the mystery of the will of God, that he might gather together in one all things in Christ, which are both in heaven and on earth, even in him.* [87]

This is the man and no other who is the subject for

the argument of theology; such is the essence which is at once a principle for a richer investigation than is possible to philosophy and a datum which cannot be resolved into the rational evidence.

Since grace builds on nature we can move from the supernatural truth revealed to faith to the natural truth it implies; for instance, what is due to human nature as such and to human nature in a connatural state can be inferred and even enlarged on from the man *who shall change our vile body, that it may be fashioned like unto his glorious body, according to the working whereby he is able to subdue all things unto himself.* [88] The discourse can move from what is explicitly and actually revealed in the living Scriptures and stated in the articles of faith to truths implicitly and virtually present. Moreover the movement is descensive, *per viam judicii*, according to the wisdom of resolving the lower in the higher, not ascensive, *per via inventionis*, according to the science of discovering causes from effects. [89]

Next, the datum which is the basis of reasoning is different in philosophy and in theology. In philosophy it is a necessary truth manifested in experience, a reflection, as the scholastics say, of the divine intellect rather than of a divine decree, whereas for theology it is a manifold made by God's free power and mercy, *according to his good pleasure which he hath purposed in himself in the dispensation of the fulness of time.* [90] What is first given is less the moral to be drawn than the story of his mighty saving deeds in history, and the mystery of his calling us through suffering to the sharing of his own happiness. Though St Thomas again and again seeks to display, sometimes subtly and profoundly, sometimes superficially and plainly, how right and proper the whole operation is in all its details, he never for a moment thinks that these arguments *ex convenientiis* bring out a strict necessity in the providential plan. The only necessity known to theology lies in the logic of drawing necessary conclusions from what is freely given.

His guiding theological principle is stated at the beginning of his treatise on the Incarnation; *those things which come to pass by the sole will of God above all that is due to creatures cannot become known to us except inasmuch as they are delivered in Holy Scripture, through which the divine will is declared to us.* [92] To this free act of God man's free act of faith is the response, and it is from this, ruled by no necessity of internal evidence such as appears in the understanding of first principles and the science of conclusions, [93] that Christian theology develops. Despite procedural resemblances between them, notable in some scholastic writings, theology and philosophy are different in kind, not only because theology is supernatural by its object, but because this object is a gift that could never have been anticipated from looking at what we are by nature.

On this account its discourse is richer than that of metaphysical philosophy which, starting from abstract meanings, must confine its argumentation by inclusion to what they imply, and can touch on physical attributes only by the connexive argumentation proper to the natural sciences, that is by working from the fact that two objects are constantly or repeatedly observed to be associated together. [94] Theology, on the other hand, does not start from a pure meaning but from the revelation of God in his deeds; its evidence is not the level light of the intelligibility of being in the third degree of abstraction but the subtler and more particular and pervasive perceptions of the Spirit; and its scientific argumentation by inclusion or implication will not be restricted to timeless and spaceless meanings about man but can make explicit and actual whatever is implicitly and virtually contained in the history of humanity, created, fallen, redeemed, and restored in Christ. It works not with ideal humanity but with the perfect man, with the perfection of species, mode, and order, that is of specific completeness, integrity, and right bearing to purpose. [95] The revelation is not of merely natural humanity adapted to some fictional environment, but is centered on a man who was held back from his transfiguration only by his choosing to bear our ills for love of us. [96]

"CAUSE" IN THEOLOGICAL DISCOURSE

The same combined likeness and unlikeness between philosophical and theological reasonings which we have just noticed in the passage from "essence" to attribute also appears when the passage is looked at in terms of causality. As already noticed, at the heart of *scientia* lies the conviction that effects depend on their proper causes, not only for their being, but also for their being understood.

"Cause" is an analogical concept with no one fixed degree and kind of meaning, and is divided, with regard to physical things, into the four categories of efficient cause, *agens*, the producer of the effect, the material cause, *causa materialis*, the subject of the effect, the formal cause, *causa formalis*, the shaping idea within the effect, and the final cause, *finis*, the purpose of the effect. [98] This rough division will be refined and treated with more detail during the course of the *Summa* in considering, for instance, the causality of participation whereby perfections discovered in this world can be attributed to God, the creative activity of God, the motions of divine grace, the operation of multiple causes within this world-order, and the teleology of human activity. For the present it will serve our purpose if we stay with the general meaning which applies to efficient, formal, and final causes, and take it as a real and positive principle on which "another" depends for its being and for its being understood. The situation is one of dependence, of this being because of that, not merely of observed sequences, of this following that.

This "another" may be diverse from the first, or really distinct from the first, or conceptually distinct (distinctive) though really identical. Let us confine our attention to an effect that is a diverse thing from the cause and an effect that exhibits a distinctive meaning contrasting with the cause. Corresponding to these the scholastics draw the distinction between a 'physical' cause and a 'metaphysical' cause. Now a metaphysical cause contains the effect, not just the ability of producing it; in reality the two are identified, so that if the first is posited the 'other' necessarily follows. [100] The nexus between them is internal. Posit the existence of a physical cause, however, and the effect can ot be deduced as happening or as going to happen; the cause may be a free agent, able to do something yet not doing it, or it may by an operating cause yet not in fact producing its effect, like the fire when the three holy children were cast into the furnace. [101] In this case the nexus between cause and effect is not that of the internal relationship of the two terms taken alone, but is wrought also of many external factors the presence of which can be certified only by observation of fact.

This is the work of the natural sciences, which have their own methods of determining the meaning and incidence of natural laws. Metaphysical philosophy must confine its argumentation from cause to effect to cases where the effect is conceptually distinct from the cause, but in reality identical, as when from immutable being it infers eternal being, and from spiritual being it infers immortal being. Notice, in passing, that this limitation does not apply to argumentation from effect to cause, when, on effect being posited as a real object and one requiring explanation, it is recognized to lack sufficient reason within itself for its existence, and this therefore is looked for outside in a diverse thing.

Now the "cause" posited for Christian theology is not a unified system of necessary reasons discovered in experience and implying metaphysical causation in the abstract, but a much richer and concrete complex. We should leave such terminology and go to the Bible instead-it is the presence of God with his people, the revelation of the Son in whom the Father was well pleased and the dwelling of the Spirit in our hearts. The limbs of Christ's body stretch over the whole world: accept this, and then, to return to the logic of argumentation, so much more can be inferred by the method of inclusion and implication than were the mystery of the Lord isolated in the manner of a supreme metaphysical cause.

You might think that nothing could be more comprehensive than the *causa universalis* of St Thomas's philosophical theology, and that the personal God there inferred, who is no absentee from the universe he creates and directs in every detail, is more divine than the God who may be discovered in Plato and Aristotle. Even so, for all the wonder and worship evoked, he is not yet the *God who so loved the world as to give his only begotten Son*, [102] and whose particular providence extends to things for which philosophy has little regard. *Are not five sparrows sold for two farthings, and not one of them is forgotten before God?* [103]

Philosophical theology enters into the substance of the Summa; its arguments, however, are the ground-bass to the movement of *sacra doctrina*, not the whole. Otherwise the Summa would be like other works of human wisdom, a statement of the conflict between essence and existence, a protest of men confined within themselves, perhaps a plea for reason and dignity. An undercurrent from the tragic sense of life in the poets and philosophers runs through the Summa, but their experience has moved into a new dimension. The same phenomena remain and the natures they manifest are not obliterated. The ideas are not shadowed by the appearance, as for the Platonists; the logos is not remote from sensibility, as for the Stoics; the touch of divinity is not rare, like the good fortune of Eudemian Ethics. The Word is made flesh and has come into history, and now meaning and deed are conjoined, *sacramentum* is translated into *res*, [105] creatures are real as both things and signs, [106 and as real they are held in God in whose Image they are both expressed and created. [107] The feelings that stir are taken into the charity which is the root, mother, and mover of all fair love, [108] the sevenfold Gift of the Spirit is not a stroke of genius but a permanent condition, [109] for the Son and the Spirit are sent to God's people and have taken up their abode, [110] and the kingdom of heaven is already with us though we have yet to rejoice in its glory. This is the reality, compact of time and eternity, bearing still the wounds received on earth and transfigured in heaven, this is the *causa* for the knowledge of the blessed from which *sacra doctrina* derives. So then, to beat back again to the logic of inclusion and implication, you will apprehend how much wider is the area of maneuver and how much deeper the grounds of inference for theology than for philosophy. The reasoning can be no less strict, the development no less homogeneous, yet the process has so much more to go on; the being on whom all is centered is not just a necessary reason but God who has descended into hell and conquered the last enemy, and now possesses every shade, every twist, every particularity of every creature.

At the beginning of this science there is God as God, not merely first being; at the ending there is the vision of himself, not the felicity of contemplating the reasons for things; and in between there are the works of redemption, *opera reparationis*, freely given and freely to be accepted, less meanings to be expected than things that have been done and are being done for us. [112] Faith takes the whole, deed and meaning, and its teaching is that of both a prophecy-religion and a wisdom-religion. Further, re-enacting the mysteries is part of its teaching, for liturgy and the dogmas go together: St Thomas speaks of explicit faith in the mysteries of Christ, especially with respect to the things the Church universally solemnizes and officially publishes. [113]

There are phases in its causal arguments when theology treats of metaphysical causality; thus, eternity is inferred from immutability, [113] and immortality from spirituality. [114] Yet much more than perpetuity and deathlessness are included, for eternity and immortality as considered by theology are taken into the life of the blessed Trinity, [115] and related to the resurrection of Christ. [116] Similarly the problem of evil is lifted from the level of mainly rational treatment [117] to the mystery of sin. [118] Original sin is not an anthropological postulate to explain our flawed nature but a penalty that is a revealed truth, as also is its annulment by the life, death, and resurrection of Christ. [119] Examples could easily be multiplied to show that the Summa is moving, and with assurance, in a world of causes and effects beyond the reach of metaphysical and natural philosophy.

The arguments of Christian theology are conducted according to the principle of virtual inclusion so long as they remain within the *revelabile*, and conversely they remain within the *revelabile* so long as they do not go off into purely private speculation or introduce elements from outside the deposit of faith. Such para-theological studies will earn the respect to which they are entitled; they may even be officially recommended as profitable for devotion, all the same they do not belong to *our common salvation* through the *faith once delivered through the saints*, [120] or to the development of truths of the Christian revelation.

BEYOND LOGIC

It can be objected that such a logical consideration as the principle of virtual inclusion is irrelevant and perhaps even irreverent when applied to the living mind of the body of Christ. Is it not to treat Christ as the middle term of a third-figure syllogism? Christ is man, Christ is God, therefore God is man.

Recall however that argumentations of this kind have a venerable history. Nobody pretends that a systematized theology is conterminous with *sacra doctrina*, yet there have been times when the Church in order to maintain the identity of its teaching has engaged itself with the logic of predication and the terms of highly speculative philosophy; and, it may be added, the simple people have sometimes scented the right formula more correctly than many of the experts.

Two classical instances of orthodoxy striving for correct logical formulation are the περιχώρησις, of St John Damascene, or *circumincessio* or reciprocal inexistence and compenetration of the three Persons of the blessed Trinity, which governs usage of the personal and essential names for the divine trinity in unity, [122] and the ἀντίδοσις, or *communicatio idiomatum*, the exchange of divine and human attributes in the person of Christ. [123]

All the faithful, simple and learned, agree in the same thing, and rough speech agrees with a finer grained technique once this is authoritatively approved as the touchstone of orthodoxy. All *are baptized in one Spirit into one body*, [124] all have *one mind in Christ*, [125] *but there are diversities of graces, though the same spirit, to one indeed by the spirit the word of wisdom, and to another the word of knowledge according to the same spirit.* [126] And for the theologian it is especially the word of knowledge, *scientia*, which, St Thomas notes, enters into secondary causes and public teaching. [127]

Ultimate Christian truth is beyond our expression. *We speak the wisdom of God in a mystery, which is hidden, which God ordained before the world, unto our glory, which none of the princes of this world knew, for if they had known it they would never have crucified the Lord of glory.* [128] Nevertheless it is without apology and because of no regrettable necessity that the Church takes this mystery into the realm of human meanings; for we should present to God *a reasonable service*, [129] and *bring into captivity every understanding unto the obedience of Christ.* [130] God's people ask questions, and they are answered in the medium of their question, sometimes to rule out heresy, sometimes to bring out the teaching of faith into our light. [131]

That the processes of systematic theology are not merely analyses of meaning has already been indicated; they start from a cleaving to God by faith, and the force of that existential affirmation persists throughout the discourse. Moreover, in some particular cases they may start from the established practices with which they are faced. The reasons they develop may even strike some as retrospective, in the sense that the fact is first accepted, and then rationalized; thus a theologian may argue from the Church's custom of infant baptism to infer the presence of Original Sin, [133] and from the Church's law to infer that children should not be baptized against the will of their parents, [134] from the Church's liturgy to show that bread and wine no longer remain after the eucharistic consecration, [135] and from the Church's practice to infer the Pope's prerogative of editing the creed. [136] Similarly the question of the ordination of women is ruled by prescription rather than by speculative reason. St. Thomas lays down the guiding principle; *the Church's custom has the greatest authority, and in all matters we should match it, for the doctrine itself of the Catholic Doctors derives its authority from the Church, and therefore we should take our stand there rather than with Augustine or Jerome or any other doctor whatever.* [137]

Nor are the dialectical processes themselves merely exercises in disinterested curiosity. For the Church consults the piety and devotion of the faithful which may move ahead of pure scholarship and speculation. They have received the Spirit to know the things of God though they may not speak the learned words of human wisdom. [138] *Lex orandi est lex credendi*, and liturgy is a source of doctrine, whereas logic is no more than ritual, a rule of procedure. And if the science of the theologian rises to wisdom, this will not be merely the intellectual virtue of taking a comprehensive view but the Gift of the Spirit which knows because it is in love. [139] It is doubtful whether in history the advance of any science can be represented merely as a growth of ideas, for scientists themselves have their loyalties and their own poetry; it is certain that instructed devotion is the spring of every advance in real theology. Yet the advance is by reasoning, if only, as Richard of St Victor said when defending himself against those who criticized his application of logic to the mysteries, like Balaam's ass who first saw the angel in the path and was beaten for her part in declaring the mysteries. [140]

ENDNOTES

[2]: Romans 8:18

[3]: Ephesians 4:5

[4]:   QDeVer.Q14.A12,   ST.III.Q64.A2, Sent.IV.D17.Q3.A1.Q5

[a]: *Editors Note:* Fr. Gilby originally includes "who himself had not arrived at the Church's teaching on the Immaculate Conception."

[5]: ST.I.Q32.A2.Rep1

[6]: Galatians 1:18, Apocalypse 22:18

[7]: *Dei Filius*, ch. 4; *Commonitorium*, 23, 3

[13]: Sent.III.D25.Q2.A2, *Whether the faith progresses over the succession of time*; QDeVer.Q14.A12, *Is there one faith for moderns and ancients*; ST.II-II.Q1.A7, *Whether the articles of faith have increased in course of time?*

[14]: ST.II-II.Q1.A1-2

[15]: ST.I.Q1.A3, 7

[16]: Hebrews 11:6

[17]: ST.II-II.Q1.A7

[20]: Ibid.

[21]: ST.I-II.Q107.1-3

[22]: Sent.III.D25.Q2.A2.qa1.ad5

[24]: ibid.

[27]: ST.I.Q75.A4
[29]: ST.I.Q76.A8
[32]: QDeVer.Q14.A12
[33]: QDeVer.Q14.A12.Rep3
[34]: Sent.III.D24.Q1.A1.qa2.ad5
[35]: John 1:16
[36]: 1 John 2:2
[37]: Ephesians 1:19-22
[38]: ST.I.Q14.A15.Rep3
[39]: Sent.III.D24.Q1.A2.qa2.ad2
[40]: 1 Corinthians 2:5; ST.II-II.Q1.A1
[41]: Romans 1:16
[42]: Hebrews 12:2
[43]: ST.I.Q32.A4
[44]: ST.II-II.Q11.A1
[45]: ST.II-II.Q11.A2
[46]: Sent.IV.D13.Q2.A1; ST.II-II.Q11.A2.Rep3
[48]: Sent.III.D25.Q2.A1.qa3; ST.II-II.Q1.A9.Rep1
[49]: 1 Corinthians 3:22

[b]: *Editors note*, an example of this would be St. Paul VI's *Humanae Vitae* which judges on the matter of contraception or St. Paul II's *Evangelium Vitae* which judges on abortion, although they are matters of natural law. Another famous example surrounds condemnations of laxism and rigorism by the Church, cf., Harty, John. "Probabilism." The Catholic Encyclopedia. Vol. 12. New York: Robert Appleton Company, 1911.

[53]: ST.I.Q1.A3
[54]: ST.I.Q1.A1
[55]: ST.I.Q1.A2.Rep2

[56]: ST.I.Q1.A4

[57]: ST.I.Q1.A5.Rep2

[58]: ST.I.Q1.A6

[59]: ST.I.Q1.A7

[60]: ST.I.Q1.A8

[61]: ST.I.Q1.A9

[62]: ST.I.Q1.A10

[63]: ST.I.Q27.A1 for Nicea; ST.III.Q35.A4 for Ephesus; ST.III.Q18.A1 for Constantinople II

[66]: ST.III.Q25.A2

[67]: ST.I.Q16.A2

[69]: ST.I.Q3.A8.Rep3; ST.I.Q30.A3; Metaph.Bk5.L12

[70]: ST.I.Q75.A2.Rep1; Metaph.Bk8.L2

[71]: Thus the plurality of perfections in God's simple being, ST.I.Q13.A4, and the coincidence of his justice and mercy, ST.I.Q21.A4

[72]: Thus the subject and predicate in a tautology, or the circumstance of translation. Cf., ST.I.Q33.A1, for the Father as *cause* in Greek and *principle* in Latin

[c]: *Editors note*, It is easy to misunderstand what is being said here by Fr. Gilby. He is **not** saying that the explication of terms (what Fr. Sola calls the *first degree of doctrinal development*) in order to clarify our terminology is **not** included in the evolution of dogma (to go from "Christ is a man" to "Christ is a rational animal" is not nothing). Rather, he is saying that, contrary to the belief of some (famously, Fr. Schultes and Fr. Garrigou-Lagrange following the *Salmanticenses*), this is not **all** that the evolution of dogma is.

[d]: *Editors note*, this is said against Lugo and Suarez

who altered the meaning of the term *virtual* as to go beyond the ordinary meaning to include truths that are *really* distinct from the revealed data.

[73]: DeTrin.C2.Q6.A1

[74]: Sent.I.Q1.9: "I respond that there are two ways to add to it: by adding something contrary to or diverse from it--and this is an error and presumptuous--or by adding something that is implicitly contained in it, by expounding it--and this is praiseworthy."

[75]: ST.I.Q3.A5; ST.I.Q31.A2.Rep2

[76]: ST.I.Q1. A.3, 7

[78]: ST.II-II.Q8.A1.Rep2

[79]: ST.II-II.Q1.A7

[80]: DeTrin.Q2.A2.13

[81]: ST.I.Q3.A3; ST.I.Q29.A2.Rep3; Metaph.Bk7.L5

[82]: DeCael

[83]: ST.I.Q8.A2.Rep3

[84]: ST.I.Q76.A8; ST.I.Q77.A1.Rep1; ST.II-II.Q48.A1; ST.II-II.Q80.A1

[85]: John 1:14-16

[86]: Colossians 2:10

[87]: Ephesians 1:10

[88]: Philippians 3:21

[89]: ST.I.Q79.A8-9

[90]: Ephesians 1:9

[92]: ST.III.Q1.A3

[93]: ST.II-II.Q1.A4-5

[95]: ST.I.Q5.A5

[96]: ST.III.Q15.A4; ST.III.Q45.A2

[98]: SCG3.C10; ST.I.Q105.A5;

[100]: Metaph.Bk5.L1
[101]: Daniel 3
[102]: John 3:16
[103]: Luke 12:6
[105]: ST.III.Q60.A2; ST.III.Q65.A3; ST.III.Q73.A3; ST.III.Q79.A1
[106]: ST.I.Q45.A3, 4, 7; ST.I.Q79.A1
[107]: ST.I.Q15.A3; ST.I.Q34.A3; ST.I.Q35.A2; ST.I.Q44.A3
[108]: ST.II-II.Q23.A8
[109]: ST.I-II.Q68.A1-3
[110]: ST.I.Q43.A3, 5
[111]: ST.I.Q1.A1.Rep2
[112]: ST.II-II.Q2.A7
[113]: ST.I.Q10.A2
[114]: ST.I.Q75.A9
[115]: ST.I.Q10.A3
[116]: ST.III.Q56.A1
[117]: ST.I.Q48-9
[118]: ST.I-II.Q79
[119]: ST.I-II.Q81-83; ST.III.Q48-49; ST.III.Q50.A6
[120]: Jude 3
[122]: ST.I.Q39
[123]: ST.III.Q16
[124]: 1 Corinthians 12:13
[125]: 1 Corinthians 2:6
[126]: 1 Corinthians 12:4-8
[127]: ST.II-II.Q9.A2; ST.II-II.Q177.A2
[128]: 1 Corinthians 2:7-8
[129]: Romans 12:1
[130]: 2 Corinthians 10:5

[131]: Sent.III.D23.Q1.A2.Rep3
[133]: SCG4.C50
[134]: ST.II-II.Q10.A12
[135]: ST.III.Q75.A2
[136]: ST.II-II.Q1.A10
[137]: ST.II-II.Q10.A12
[138]: 1 Corinthians 2:12-13
[139]: ST.I.Q1.A5.Rep3; ST.I-II.Q57.A2; ST.II-II.Q45.A1.Rep2
[140]: *De Trinitate* III

Printed in Great Britain
by Amazon